MARVELOUS MAP ACTIVI

FOR YOUNG LEARNERS

Easy Reproducible Activities That Introduce Important Map and Geography Skills—and Help Kids Explore Their Neighborhood, Community, and Beyond

by Minnie Ashcroft

SCHOLASTIC
PROFESSIONAL BOOKS

NEW YORK   TORONTO   LONDON   AUCKLAND   SYDNEY
MEXICO CITY   NEW DELHI   HONGKONG   BUENOS AIRES

Dedication

For Nelle

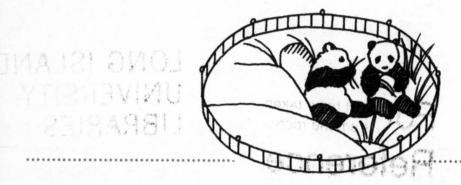

Cover design by Josué Castilleja
Interior design by Béatrice Schafroth
Illustrations by Kathie Kelleher

ISBN 0-439-17887-8
Copyright © 2002 by Minnie Ashcroft
All rights reserved.
Printed in the U.S.A.
1 2 3 4 5 6 7 8 9 10   40   08 07 06 05 04 03 02 01

TABLE OF CONTENTS

INTRODUCTION

Whether we realize it or not, we use geography every day—from reading an address on a building to planning which route to take when shopping.

Marvelous Map Activities for Young Learners opens up the fascinating world of geography to children. Using fun and engaging activities and games that can be played individually, in small groups, or in a whole-class setting, this book provides a clear introduction to and reinforcement of basic geography skills.

The book starts out by introducing geography vocabulary to students. Children learn how to write and spell these words by creating a mini-book of geography words, completing a word search, playing bingo, and more. By repeatedly working with these words, students become more familiar with them and learn their definitions. Other games and activities also help teach students how to identify map symbols, recognize various landforms and bodies of water, understand cardinal directions, read a map of the United States, navigate neighborhood maps, and more.

Encourage students to do these activities throughout the year to explore and reinforce geography skills. The activities will also help you assess children's knowledge and progress. By the end of the year, your students will be world-class geographers.

"MY GEOGRAPHY WORDS" MINI-BOOK

Objective
To recognize geography words and practice writing these words using lowercase letters

 **Materials**

◆ **My Geography Words (pages 7–8)**

◆ **Scissors**

◆ **Pencil for each child**

◆ **Stapler**

Before You Start

1. Make double-sided copies of "My Geography Words" for each student, making sure both sides of the page line up. You can either assemble the mini-books for students, or show them how to do it. (See "To Do.")

2. Review the alphabet with students. On the board, write the letter A in uppercase and lowercase. Ask a volunteer to come up and circle the uppercase letter A. Then have another volunteer come up and draw a line under the lowercase letter.

3. Tell students that they are going to learn some geography words. Explain that *geography* is the study of Earth and the way people, plants, and animals live on and use it.

To Do

1. Give each student a copy of "My Geography Words." If you haven't already assembled the mini-books for them, show students how to do it. First, cut across the dashed lines. Then, place page 3 of the mini-book behind page 1. Finally, fold both pages along the solid line to complete the mini-book. Help students staple their mini-books together.

2. Together, read aloud the words on each page of the mini-book. You may want to discuss each word and the picture that accompanies it.

3. When you're done reading the book, ask students to go back to page 2 of the mini-book. Point out that the geography words are written in uppercase letters. Ask them to rewrite the word on the lines below each word using lowercase letters.

Going Further

Invite students to create their own geography flash cards. Have them write each geography word on a separate index card. Then have them cut out pictures of their words from magazines or newspapers. Tell them to paste their pictures on the other side of the cards. Students can use their flash cards to quiz each other in class or practice with an adult at home.

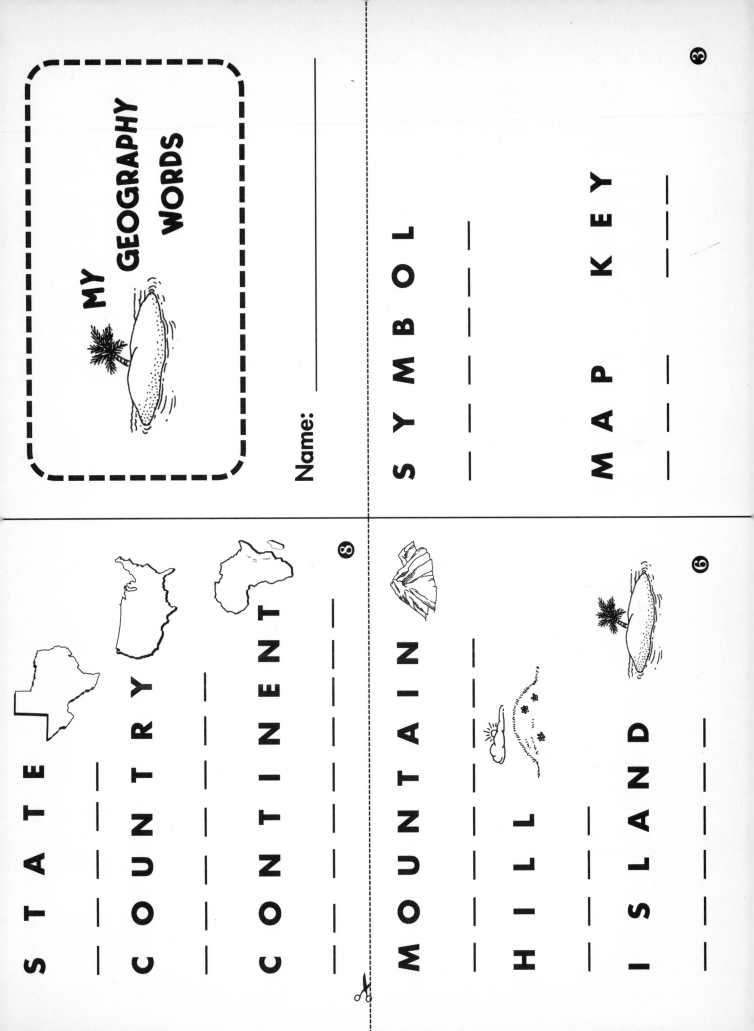

MY
GEOGRAPHY
WORDS

Name: _____

S Y M B O L

— | — | — | —

M A P   K E Y

— | — | — | —

③

S T A T E

— | — | — | —

C O U N T R Y

— | — | — | —

C O N T I N E N T

— | — | — | —

⑧

M O U N T A I N

— | — | — | —

H I L L

— | — | — | —

I S L A N D

— | — | — | —

⑥

M A P

| |

G L O B E

| |

④ ②

C O M P A S S   R O S E

N O R T H

| |

| |

S O U T H

| |

| |

L A K E

| |

| |

R I V E R

| |

| |

O C E A N

| |

| |

E A S T

| |

| |

W E S T

| |

| |

⑤ ⑦

SCRAMBLED GEOGRAPHY

Objective
To reinforce letter recognition and the spelling of geography words

Materials

◆ **Scrambled Geography Words (pages 10–11)**

◆ **Scissors**

◆ **Letter-size envelope for each student**

◆ **Pictures of the geography words (cut from magazines, newspapers, or picture books)**

Before You Start

1. Make several copies of Scrambled Geography Words, so that each student has at least one word.

2. Cut apart each word into individual letters and place each word in an envelope. For younger students, you may want to write the geography word on the outside of the envelope.

3. Cut out pictures of the vocabulary words from magazines or newspapers. You may wish to paste each picture to a piece of construction paper to make it sturdy.

4. Hold up the pictures one at a time and call on volunteers to identify them. As students correctly identify the pictures, write the words on the board. Explain to students that these words are geography words.

5. Tell students that they will play a game in which they'll unscramble some letters to form geography words.

To Do

1. Pass out an envelope to each student. Tell students that inside each envelope are the letters that make up one of the geography words on the board. Explain that their job is to put the letters in order to make up the word.

2. After students complete their words, have them raise their hand and read their word aloud to you.

3. Have students switch envelopes with a partner. Keep playing until students become proficient at spelling these words.

Literature Link

***The Armadillo from Amarillo* by Lynne Cherry (Harcourt Brace, 1994).**
An armadillo named Sasparillo leaves his home in San Antonio to learn about the geography and environment of Texas.

SCRAMBLED GEOGRAPHY WORDS

M	A	P						
G	L	O	B	E				
S	Y	M	B	O	L			
M	A	P	K	E	Y			
C	O	M	P	A	S	S		
C	O	N	T	I	N	E	N	T
C	O	U	N	T	R	Y		
S	T	A	T	E				
M	O	U	N	T	A	I	N	
H	I	L	L					

SCRAMBLED GEOGRAPHY WORDS

V	A	L	L	E	Y

P	L	A	I	N

C	A	N	Y	O	N

I	S	L	A	N	D

P	E	N	I	N	S	U	L	A

L	A	K	E

R	I	V	E	R

O	C	E	A	N

G	U	L	F

B	A	Y

FIND A GEOGRAPHY WORD

Objective
To find and circle geography words in a word search puzzle

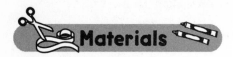

Materials

◆ **Geography Word Search (page 13)**

◆ **Pencil for each student**

Before You Start

1. Write the following letters on the board, leaving an equal amount of space between each letter:

N O T A C **N O R T H** B E

2. Ask students if they can spot the geography word in this row of letters. Have a volunteer come up and circle the word **NORTH.**

3. Explain that you are going to pass out a word search that contains geography words hidden amid other letters. Tell students that they must locate the words listed at the top of the page and circle them in the grid.

To Do

1. Give each student a copy of the Geography Word Search and a pencil. If you want, you can set a time limit based on students' individual abilities.

2. If students do not complete their work, have them finish the word search at home. If a child is having difficulty, ask him or her to have an adult help at home.

Answer

Name: _____

GEOGRAPHY WORD SEARCH

Find and circle the following words in the puzzle below.
The words may go up, down, across, or backward.

**NORTH SOUTH EAST WEST RIVER OCEAN LAKE HILL
MOUNTAIN PLAIN ISLAND COUNTRY MAP EARTH GLOBE**

```
I  X  J  W  T  A  R  G  Y  R  T  N  U  O  C
P  O  C  E  R  B  H  S  H  I  L  L  D  E  F
H  Y  D  S  G  Q  I  W  T  C  U  F  W  N  B
N  O  R  T  H  U  C  L  X  V  D  B  E  E  Z
C  F  B  O  P  A  N  I  S  L  A  N  D  P  Y
A  M  L  G  V  K  J  Y  W  J  M  Z  X  A  S
K  O  B  L  M  I  E  A  S  T  I  V  F  P  O
H  U  K  E  O  C  M  G  R  W  H  M  J  Q  U
D  N  O  Z  C  F  S  X  N  D  U  A  O  K  T
G  T  F  R  E  V  I  R  U  E  V  P  M  W  H
J  A  I  H  A  Y  S  G  L  O  B  E  R  L  O
R  I  E  D  N  T  N  B  K  Q  N  M  P  L  V
A  N  B  G  Q  A  J  Z  T  N  I  A  L  P  N
Q  C  H  T  R  A  E  U  S  S  K  T  V  L  M
H  I  Q  P  R  Z  R  O  Y  L  A  K  E  X  U
```

Going Further

Have students make up their own word search puzzle using words that they know. You can write a list of words on the board that students have recently learned from a story. Have them choose some or all of the words and write them at the top of a piece of paper. Then have them create their own puzzles. Invite students to exchange puzzles with a partner or take them home to present to an adult.

Name: _____

GEOGRAPHY WORD SEARCH

Find and circle the following words in the puzzle below.
The words may go up, down, across, or backward.

**NORTH SOUTH EAST WEST RIVER OCEAN LAKE HILL
MOUNTAIN PLAIN ISLAND COUNTRY MAP EARTH GLOBE**

I X J W T A R G Y R T N U O C

P O C E R B H S H I L L D E F

H Y D S G Q I W T C U F W N B

N O R T H U C L X V D B E E Z

C F B O P A N I S L A N D P Y

A M L G V K J Y W J M Z X A S

K O B L M I E A S T I V F P O

H U K E O C M G R W H M J Q U

D N O Z C F S X N D U A O K T

G T F R E V I R U E V P M W H

J A I H A Y S G L O B E R L O

R I E D N T N B K Q N M P L V

A N B G Q A J Z T N I A L P N

Q C H T R A E U S S K T V L M

H I Q P R Z R O Y L A K E X U

KNOW WHAT I MEAN?

Objective
To reinforce geography vocabulary words and their definitions

 Materials

◆ **Geography Word Cards (pages 15–16)**

◆ **Geography Definition Cards (pages 17–18)**

◆ **Scissors**

Before You Start

1. Decide whether you want to use all 24 geography words and definitions on pages 15–18. You may want to pick only words that your students are already familiar with.

2. This game requires an even number of players. There are enough cards for 24 players. If there are more than 24 players, you may wish to photocopy some words and definitions more than once.

3. Tell students that geography is the study of Earth and the way people, plants, and animals live on and use it. Knowing geography helps people learn about the land and water in their neighborhood and community.

4. Explain that there are vocabulary words that will help them to understand and talk about geography. Recognizing these words and their definitions will help them become better geographers.

To Do

1. Give each student a word or a definition.

2. When you say "Go," have each student walk around the room looking for the player with the definition or word that matches his or hers. The first pair to sit down wins.

Other Ways to Play

✔ For students who have a visual learning style, or for students whose primary language is not English, you may wish to create another set of cards that have pictures of the vocabulary words instead of the definition. Play the game with vocabulary words and pictures.

✔ As students become more familiar with the vocabulary words and pictures, add the definitions. The first three players who match the correct word, definition, and picture and sit down are the winners.

 14

GEOGRAPHY WORD CARDS

Geography	Canyon
Globe	Compass rose
Grid map	Continent
Hill	Country
Island	Directions
Lake	Earth

GEOGRAPHY WORD CARDS

Plain	Landform
River	Map
Route	Map key
State	Mountain
Symbol	Ocean
Valley	Peninsula

the study of Earth and the way people, plants, and animals live on and use it	very deep valley
a model of Earth	it shows directions on a map
a map divided by lines that form squares used to find places	a very large body of land
land that is higher than the land around it	a land and the people who live there
land that has water all around it	they help you find places on a map or globe; north, east, south, west
body of water with land all around it	our world

GEOGRAPHY DEFINITION CARDS

flat land	a kind of land, such as a plain, hill, or mountain
long body of water that flows across the land	a drawing of a place
a way of going from one place to another	something that tells what the symbols on a map mean
part of a country	highest kind of land
a drawing that stands for something real	very large body of salt water
low land between hills or mountains	land that has water on three sides

GEO-BINGO

Objective
To reinforce geography words and their definitions

Materials

◆ **Geo–Bingo Game Card (page 20)**

◆ **Geography Word Cards (pages 15–16)**

◆ **A bowl or large envelope**

◆ **Pencil for each child**

◆ **16 beans or markers for each child**

◆ **Pictures of the geography words (optional, cut out from magazines, newspapers, or picture books)**

Before You Start

1. List all 24 words from the Geography Word Cards on the board.

2. Call on volunteers to read each word and give a definition. You may wish to assist students in their definitions by holding up pictures of the words.

To Do

1. Give each student a copy of the Geo-Bingo Game Card. Invite students to pick 16 words from the list and copy one word into each box on their game card. (You can also copy the words on each game card beforehand.)

2. Place the Geography Word Cards into a bowl or large envelope. Pick out one word at a time and read the word aloud. You may wish to have a volunteer circle the word on the board.

3. Tell students to search their game cards for the word. If they have the word, they should place a bean or marker over it. The first player to cover four words in a row—across, up, down, or diagonally—wins.

Other Ways to Play

✔ For a shorter game of Geo–Bingo, cross out the last column up and down and the last row across the game card, leaving only nine squares.

✔ For a more challenging game, photocopy and cut apart the Geography Definition Cards (pages 17–18) and place them in a bowl or large envelope. Pick out one definition card at a time and read it aloud. Allow students time to find the geography word on their game board that corresponds to the definition. Just as in the original version, the first player to cover four words in a row wins.

Going Further

Create more geography word and definition cards to add to this game as students expand their vocabulary.

Name: _____

GEO-BINGO GAME CARD

LANDFORM MATCH

Objective
To identify different landforms and create a geography picture glossary

 **Materials**

◆ **Landform Picture Dictionary (page 22)**

◆ **Scissors**

◆ **Paste**

◆ **Crayons**

Before You Start

1. Write the following vocabulary words on the board: plain, hill, island, mountain, river, valley, lake, and ocean.

2. Call on volunteers to read each word aloud and define each word.

3. Tell students that they are going to create their own geography picture glossaries.

To Do

1. Give each student a copy of the Landform Picture Dictionary. Have them cut out the words at the bottom of the page and paste them next to the correct landform.

2. When students are finished, have them color their picture glossaries. Tell students they can refer to their geography picture glossary anytime they need to be reminded of a geography word and its picture.

Literature Links

***Ebbie & Flo* by Irene Kelly (Smith & Kraus, 1998).**
Ebbie and Flo are salmon twins. Ebbie doesn't want to leave the nest, while adventurous Flo is eager to explore the river and the deep blue sea. Ebbie and Flo ride the rapids, go over waterfalls, and have an encounter with a whale.

***Where the River Begins* by Thomas Locker (Puffin, 1993).**
Two young boys and their grandfather go on a camping trip to find the source of a river.

Name: _____

LANDFORM PICTURE DICTIONARY

Look at the picture of different kinds of land and water.
Cut out the words below and paste each one next to the part
of the picture that shows the land or water.

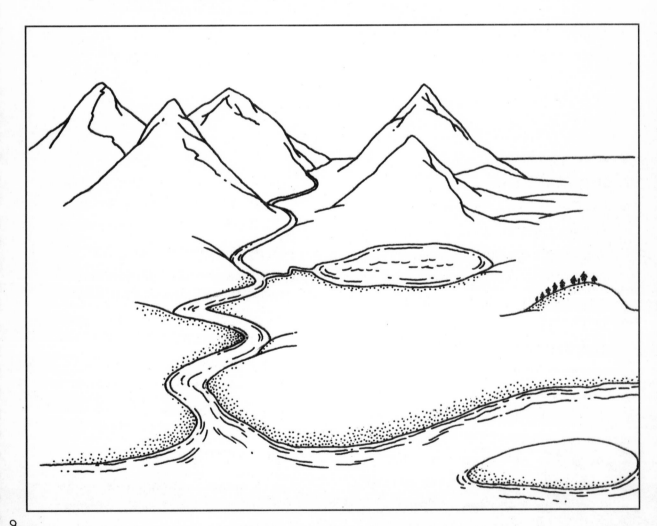

Plain	Hill	Island	Mountain
River	Valley	Lake	Ocean

GEOGRAPHY SYMBOLS SEARCH

Objective

To recognize geography words and symbols and differentiate them from other symbols

 **Materials**

- ◆ **Geography Search Grid (page 24)**
- ◆ **Crayon or pencil for each student**
- ◆ **Pictures of a compass rose, globe, lake, river, mountain, and the United States (cut out from magazines, newspapers, or picture books)**

Before You Start

1. Write the following vocabulary words on the board: compass rose, globe, lake, river, mountain, and United States. Read the words aloud as you show students matching pictures.

2. Tell students that maps often have *symbols*, or drawings that stand for something real. Explain that a symbol can be drawn for each of the words on the board.

3. Draw a picture of a mountain on the board and ask students what this symbol might stand for. Ask volunteers to come up and draw a symbol for each of the words listed on the board.

To Do

1. Give each student a copy of the Geography Search Grid and a crayon or pencil.

2. Tell students that there are 10 geography words and symbols on the page. Ask students to find and circle them. You might wish to pair up students to play this game.

3. When all students have finished, call on volunteers to name each item they circled.

Going Further

To build students' sorting skills, list the different categories of math, science, music, and reading on the board. Ask volunteers to sort the non-geography words and symbols in the grid into the various categories.

Name: _____

GEOGRAPHY SEARCH GRID

Find and circle the 10 words and symbols that have something to do with geography.

STOP	**NORTH**	**=**	**3**	(map of USA)
(pumpkin)	(volcano)	(musical note)	**SOUTH**	(key)
(mountains)	**A**	(book)	(river)	**+**
EAST	(compass)	**B**	(globe)	(island)

MATCH THE MAP SYMBOLS

Objective

To recognize map symbols and match them to the words that identify them

Materials

◆ **Matching Game Cards: Words and Symbols (pages 26–27)**

◆ **Scissors**

Before You Start

1. Photocopy a set of Matching Game Cards for each group of two or three students.

2. Tell students that maps often use symbols. Explain that a *symbol* is a drawing that stands for something real.

3. On the board, draw a picture of a traffic light. Ask students what they think this symbol stands for. Explain that a map that has symbols will also feature a map key that tells what the symbols stand for.

4. Ask students to name some symbols that might be drawn on a classroom map, a neighborhood map, or a city map. You may want to ask one or two volunteers to come to the board and draw a symbol that might be used on a map.

5. Tell students that they are going to play a memory game that uses map symbols and words.

To Do

1. Place students into groups of two or three. Give each group one set of word cards and one set of symbol cards. Explain that for every symbol card, there is a matching word card.

2. Have students shuffle all the cards and place them in rows face down on the floor.

3. Players take turns flipping over two cards to see if they match. For example, a symbol of a tree and the word "tree" match. A player who finds matching cards keeps the pair and takes another turn. If the two cards do not match, the player must turn them face down and the next player has a turn. The player who collects the most matching cards wins.

Going Further

For a more challenging game, add real-life picture cards of the words to the set of cards. You can cut out pictures from newspapers and magazines. You may want to mount them on white construction paper and trim them to match the size of the word and symbol cards. Students should shuffle and place 60 cards face down on the floor. In this version, three matching cards (picture, word, symbol) constitute a matching set.

MATCHING GAME CARDS: WORDS

Tree	Railroad	School	Post office	Bakery
Pet store	Library	Playground	Grocery store	Farm
Clothing store	Shoe store	Music store	Compass rose	Mountain
Ocean	River	Hill	Island	Globe

MATCHING GAME CARDS: SYMBOLS

MAP SYMBOLS DOMINOES

Objective

To play a game of dominoes that involves matching map symbols

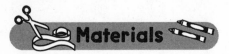 **Materials**

◆ **Symbols Dominoes (page 29)**

Before You Start

1. Photocopy a set of Symbols Dominoes for each pair of students. Cut apart the dominoes along the dashed lines.

2. Draw a picture of a mountain on the board and ask students what this symbol might stand for. Ask volunteers to come up and draw a symbol for an object such as a house, an animal, or a toy. Have them ask other students to guess what the symbol is.

3. On the board, draw the symbols from the domino cards. Review each symbol with the class. Then tell students that they are going to pair up and play a game of dominoes using these symbols.

To Do

1. Pair up students and give each pair one set of dominoes.

2. Players should place all the dominoes face down on the table. Each player picks seven dominoes. The player with the highest double domino (the piece with matching symbols in both sections) goes first.

3. The first player places his or her double domino face up on the table. Say it was the 3/3. The next player must see if he or she has any domino with 3 symbols in one section. For example, the matching domino may be the 3/6. The player should place the domino on the table with the 3 symbols end to end.

4. The first player may then match a section with 6 symbols to the 3/6 domino, or a section with 3 symbols to the 3/3 domino.

5. If a player cannot find a match from his or her dominoes, the player should pick from the remaining pile of dominoes until he or she finds a domino that will match. After the pile is used up, players who cannot match must miss a turn, or pass.

6. The game ends when one player runs out of dominoes or when neither player can match any of the remaining dominoes with those he or she still holds. The player who uses up all his or her dominoes or has the fewest number of symbols on the remaining dominoes wins.

SYMBOLS DOMINOES

LANDFORMS LEFT AND RIGHT

Objective

To use the words left and right to identify the location of geography pictures

Materials

◆ **Landforms Grid (page 31)**

◆ **Crayon or pencil for each child**

Before You Start

1. Review the concepts of left and right with students. Write the words *left* and *right* on the board. Explain that it's important to know the difference between left and right in order to understand where you are, to find things and places, or to give others directions.

2. Choose a secret location in the classroom, such as the block area, bookshelves, a learning center, or the board. Then invite a volunteer to follow your directions (e.g., go right, go left) to get to the secret location.

To Do

1. Give each student a copy of the Landforms Grid along with a crayon or a pencil.

2. Together, read the directions at the top of the page. Encourage students to look at the pictures one row at a time, crossing off the pictures according to the directions.

Answer

2 mountains (Some students may recognize that the third sentence can be answered both across from left to right as well as from top to bottom. In this case, their final answer would be 0.)

Literature Link

Water **by Frank Asch (Harcourt Brace, 1995).**
Explore the different forms of water— dew, ice, and snow —
in a tiny brook, a small pond, a large lake, a river, and an ocean.

Name: _____

LANDFORMS GRID

1. Cross off all the mountains that are to the left of a plain.
2. Cross off all the mountains that are to the right of a river.
3. Cross off all the mountains between two islands.

How many mountains remain? _____

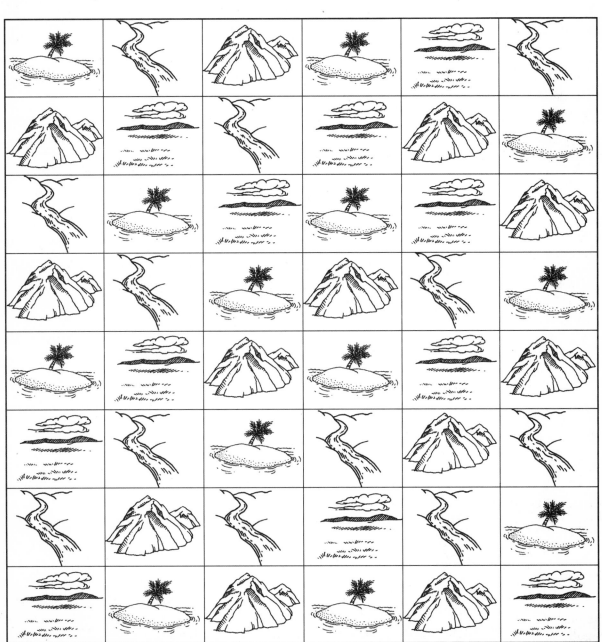

WHICH WAY DID I GO?

Objective

To locate places on a map and follow a route

 **Materials**

- ◆ **What I Saw (page 33)**
- ◆ **Where I've Been (page 34)**
- ◆ **Crayons**
- ◆ **Scissors**
- ◆ **Paste**

Before You Start

1. Tell students that a *map* is a picture that shows a detailed plan of an area to help you find places. Explain that maps often use symbols instead of words to show places.

2. Draw a picture of a house on the board and ask students what the picture represents. Invite students to think of other symbols that might appear on a map and what they would stand for, such as an animal for a zoo or a swing set for a playground.

3. Next, explain to students that a *route* is a way of going from one place to another. Tell students that in this activity, they'll look at a map and try to figure out what route a person took.

To Do

1. Give each student a copy of What I Saw. Invite them to color the pictures. Call on volunteers to identify each picture. Then have students cut out the pictures.

2. Hand out one copy of Where I've Been to each student and have them color their maps. Again, call on volunteers to identify each place on the map.

3. Have students paste the pictures from What I Saw in the correct blank box next to each place on the map.

4. Next, tell students that they are going to draw the route that was taken to visit each place. Beginning with Monday and ending with Sunday, students should draw a line from place to place.

Name: _____

WHAT I SAW

Color and cut out each picture. Then paste it next to the correct place on the map.

Monday

Tuesday

Wednesday

Thursday

Friday

Saturday

Sunday

Name: _____

Look at the map below. Paste each picture from What I Saw next to the matching place. Then draw an arrow showing the route that I followed.

FIND PIPPA

Objective

To understand the cardinal directions (north, east, south, and west) and learn how to use a compass rose

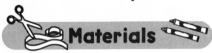 **Materials**

◆ **Where's Pippa? (page 36)**

◆ **Pencil for each child**

◆ **Globe or map of the world**

Before You Start

1. Point to the North Pole on the globe or map of the world. Tell students that the North Pole is on top of Earth. Then point to the South Pole and tell students that it is at the bottom of Earth.

2. On the board, draw a compass rose and write the four cardinal directions (north, east, south, and west) around it. Explain that a *compass rose* shows directions on a map and that these directions can help people find places on the map.

3. Explain that north is the direction toward the North Pole. Ask, "Toward which direction is the South Pole?" *(South)* Then show students that when you face north, east is to the right. Ask, "What direction is to the left?" *(West)* Note: You may want to review left and right if students have difficulty with the directions east and west.

4. Tell students that on a map, a compass rose shows the first letter of each direction. Leaving the first letter of each direction on the board, erase the remaining letters. Ask students what direction each letter stands for.

5. Tell students that they are going to answer questions on a map using a compass rose.

To Do

1. Give each student a copy of Where's Pippa? and a pencil.

2. Ask a volunteer to point out where the compass rose is located on the page. *(The upper left-hand corner)* Next, have students write the answers to the questions. When everyone is finished, review the questions and answers to assess students' understanding of cardinal directions and a compass rose.

Answers

1. north   2. west   3. east   4. south
5. hamster   6. south and west

Going Further

To reinforce students' understanding of cardinal directions, label the walls around your classroom north, south, east, and west. (Make sure the labels are placed in the correct directions.) Think of an object such as a stuffed toy or a book that is in the room. Guide a volunteer to the object using cardinal directions. When the student finds the object, let him or her think of an object in the room and guide a classmate to it using cardinal directions.

Name: _____

WHERE'S PIPPA?

Nick is looking for his cat, Pippa.
Use the compass rose to answer the questions below.

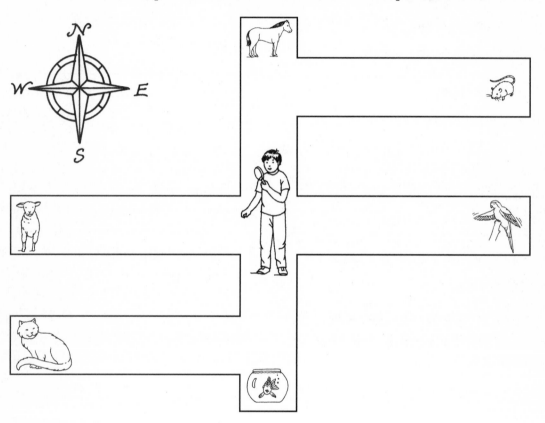

1. Is the horse north or south of Nick? _____

2. Is the lamb east or west of Nick? _____

3. Is the bird east or west of Nick? _____

4. Is the fish north or south of Nick? _____

5. What will Nick find if he walks north and then east? _____

6. What direction will Nick have to walk to find Pippa? _____

WELCOME TO THE ZOO

Objective

To understand the cardinal directions (north, east, south, and west) and use a compass rose

Materials

◆ **City Zoo Map (page 38)**

◆ **Pencil for each student**

Before You Start

1. Review the four cardinal directions (north, east, south, and west) with students.

2. Draw a compass rose on the board and label the four directions N, E, S, and W. Ask students what direction each letter stands for.

3. Tell students that they are going to answer questions about a map using a compass rose.

To Do

1. Give each student a copy of the City Zoo Map and a pencil.

2. Ask a volunteer to point out the compass rose on the City Zoo Map. Have students use the map to answer each question. Tell them to place their answers in the crossword puzzle on the page.

3. Explain that the number of each answer at the left has a corresponding number in the crossword puzzle and that students should place only one letter in each puzzle box. Note: You may want to redraw the crossword puzzle grid on the board and have volunteers come up and place the answers to the questions in the puzzle boxes.

Answers

```
          1L
      2H  I  P 3P  O  S
          O     A
          N     N
          S     D
                A
             4S  E  A  L  S
```

Literature Link

As the Roadrunner Runs by Gail Hartman (Bradbury, 1994).
Using colorful art and characters, this book introduces young readers to maps and map skills.

Name: _____

Use the map of the zoo to answer each question. Then write the answer in the crossword puzzle.

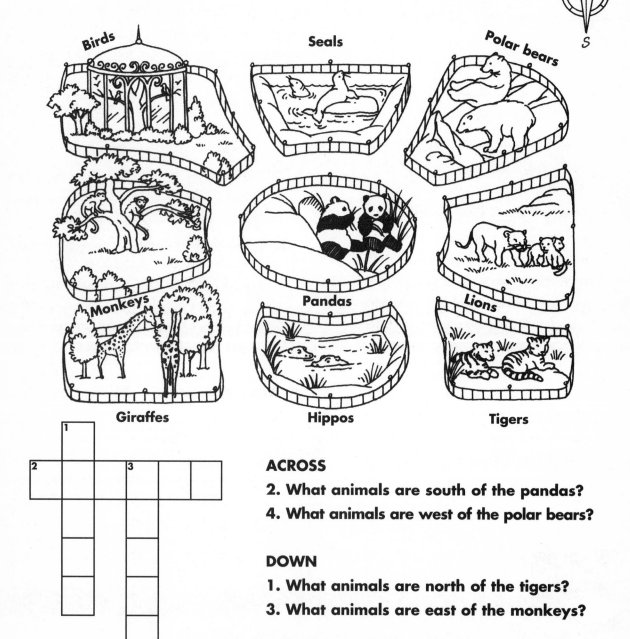

Birds   Seals   Polar bears

Monkeys   Pandas   Lions

Giraffes   Hippos   Tigers

ACROSS

2. What animals are south of the pandas?

4. What animals are west of the polar bears?

DOWN

1. What animals are north of the tigers?

3. What animals are east of the monkeys?

MATCH THE GLOBE

Objective

To recognize that Earth is made up of seven continents and four oceans

Materials

◆ **Global Mix-Up (page 40)**

◆ **Crayon or pencil for each student**

◆ **Globe or map of the world**

Before You Start

1. Show students a globe or a map of the world. Tell students that Earth is made up of land and water. Point out the large landmasses and explain that these are called *continents.*

2. List the seven continents on the board in alphabetical order: Africa, Antarctica, Asia, Australia, Europe, North America, and South America. Together with your students, read the names of the continents aloud.

3. Point out that North America is the continent on which we live. You may want to ask students to share with the class the name of the continent from which their family originally came.

4. Next, show students the bodies of water that surround the continents. Explain that these are called *oceans,* and that Earth has four of them. List the oceans on the board in alphabetical order: Arctic Ocean, Atlantic Ocean, Indian Ocean, and Pacific Ocean. Together, read the names of the oceans aloud.

To Do

1. Give each student a copy of Global Mix-Up and a crayon or pencil.

2. Tell students that the map in the upper left-hand corner shows all seven continents and all four oceans. Four of the other globes are missing some of the continents and/or oceans. Have students find and circle the only other globe with all the continents and oceans.

Going Further

Challenge more advanced students to list all the missing continents and oceans on the remaining globes.

Literature Link

Our Earth **by Anne Rockwell (Harcourt Brace, 1998).**
Discover the continents and oceans on Earth by taking a fun-filled adventure to hot deserts, snowy mountains, tropical islands, steamy rain forests, and deep oceans.

Name: _____

GLOBAL MIX-UP

Find and circle the globe that is the same as the first one.

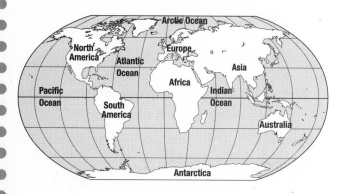

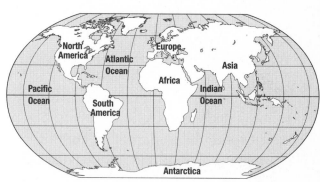

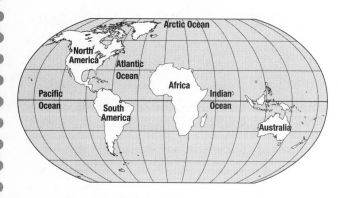

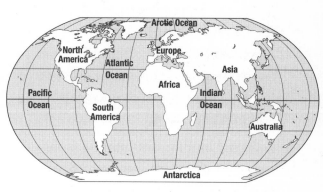

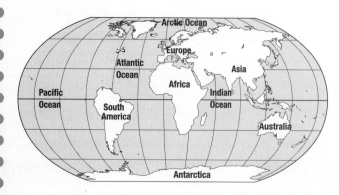

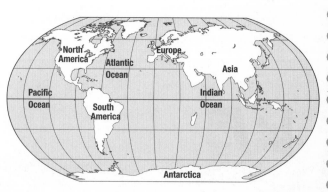

A PUZZLING MAP

Objective

To understand that a map is a drawing of a place and to recognize the shape of the United States on a map

Materials

◆ **United States Map (page 42)**

◆ **9- by 12-inch construction paper or oak tag for each student**

◆ **Paste**

◆ **Crayons**

◆ **A map of the United States**

◆ **Scissors**

Before You Start

1. Show students a map of the United States (including Alaska and Hawaii). Explain that this map shows the country in which we live.

2. Explain that the United States is made up of 50 states. Point out the lines that separate one state from another. (You may want to explain that the lines appear only on a map and not in the real world.) Point out the state in which you live.

3. Tell students that they are going to make their own puzzles of the United States. Creating these puzzles is a fun way to help them remember the shape of the country and of each state.

To Do

1. Give each student a copy of the United States map. Invite students to color their maps.

2. Have students paste their maps to construction paper or oak tag to make them sturdy.

3. Help students cut their maps into six to eight puzzle pieces. An easy way to cut the maps is into strips. Have students exchange their puzzles with a partner and challenge each other to put the map back together.

Literature Link

By a Blazing Blue Sea by S. T. Garne (Harcourt Brace, 1999).
Meet an old man, a naughty cat, and a friendly parrot who live between lush green hills and a turquoise bay on a sparkling shore.

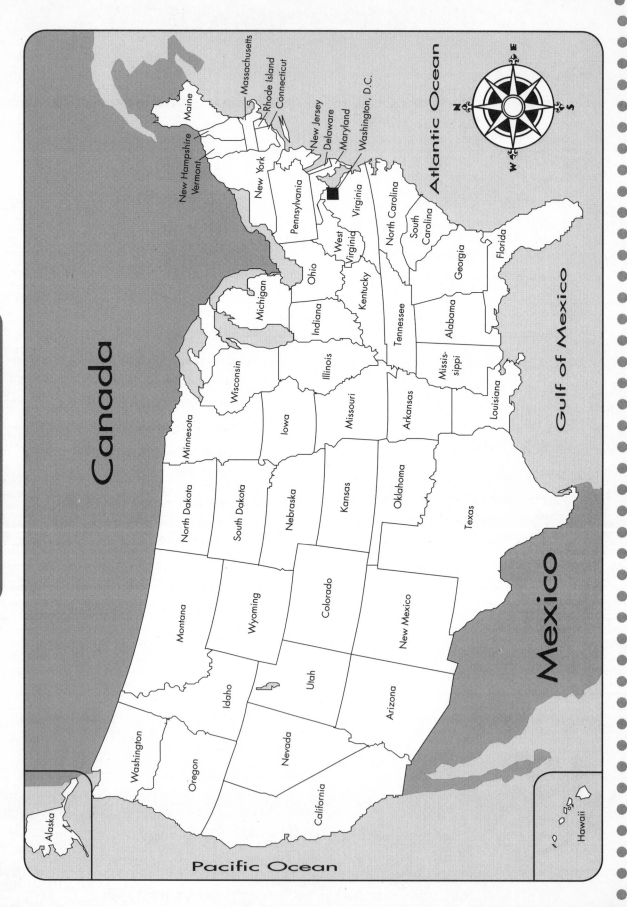

UNITED STATES MAP

Canada

Maine
New Hampshire
Vermont
Massachusetts
Rhode Island
Connecticut
New York
New Jersey
Delaware
Maryland
Washington, D.C.
Pennsylvania
West Virginia
Virginia
Ohio
North Carolina
South Carolina
Kentucky
Tennessee
Georgia
Michigan
Indiana
Illinois
Wisconsin
Missouri
Arkansas
Alabama
Mississippi
Louisiana
Florida
Iowa
Minnesota
North Dakota
South Dakota
Nebraska
Kansas
Oklahoma
Texas
Montana
Wyoming
Colorado
New Mexico
Idaho
Utah
Arizona
Washington
Oregon
Nevada
California
Alaska
Hawaii

Atlantic Ocean

Gulf of Mexico

Mexico

Pacific Ocean

WHAT STATE AM I IN?

Objective

To use the cardinal directions to locate states in the contiguous United States

Materials

◆ **State Game Cards (pages 44–47)**

◆ **Large map of the United States**

Before You Start

1. Review the four cardinal directions (north, east, south, and west) with students.

2. Draw a compass rose on the board and label the four directions N, E, S, and W. Ask students what direction each letter stands for.

3. Tell students that they are going to figure out what state they're in by using the map of the United States and their knowledge of cardinal directions.

To Do

1. Hang the map of the United States on the board or lay it flat in the center of a table.

2. Pick one of the State Game Cards and read it aloud. Ask a volunteer to come to the map and place his or her finger on the starting state. (Note: Each of the 48 contiguous states is both a starting state and an ending state in this game.) You may need to help the student find the starting state.

3. Reread the directions on the card slowly, allowing time for the student to determine the direction in which he or she is moving and count the states he or she is moving across. When the student is finished, he or she should call out the ending state's name. Continue to play the game until every student has had a turn.

Literature Link

***This Land is Your Land* by Woody Guthrie (Little Brown, 1998).**
This classic song from the 1940s is brought to life in a richly illustrated edition. Well-known folk artist Kathy Jakobsen's detailed paintings take readers on a journey across the United States, creating a memorable portrait of the diverse geography and its people.

I am in Alabama and I travel one state east and one state south. What state am I in?
(Florida)

I am in Arkansas and I travel four states east and two states north. The first letter is V. What state am I in?
(Virginia)

I am in Delaware and I travel three states south and one state west. What state am I in?
(Tennessee)

I am in California and I travel two states east and two states north. What state am I in?
(Montana)

I am in Idaho and I travel one state west and one state south. The first letter is C. What state am I in?
(California)

I am in Illinois and I travel one state east and three states south. The first letter is A. What state am I in?
(Alabama)

I am in Florida and I travel seven states north along the Atlantic Ocean. What state am I in?
(New Jersey)

I am in Colorado and I travel one state west and two states north. Then I travel three states east. What state am I in?
(Wisconsin)

I am in Arizona and I travel two states east and three states north. Then I travel one state south. The first letter is K. What state am I in?
(Kansas)

I am in Iowa and I travel two states south. What state am I in?
(Arkansas)

I am in Georgia and I travel two states west and one state south. Then I travel two states north. What state am I in?
(Missouri)

I am in Connecticut and I travel one state west and one state south. Then I travel one state west. The first letter is O. What state am I in?
(Ohio)

I am in Kansas and I travel two states west and one state north. The first letter is I. What state am I in?
(Idaho)

I am in Maryland and I travel four states south along the Atlantic Ocean. What state am I in?
(Georgia)

I am in Louisiana and I travel three states west. What state am I in?
(Arizona)

I am in Nebraska and I travel one state east. What state am I in?
(Iowa)

I am in Mississippi and I travel one state north and two states west. Then I travel three states north. What state am I in?
(South Dakota)

I am in Massachusetts and I travel one state west and one state south. The first letter is P. What state am I in?
(Pennsylvania)

I am in Kentucky and I travel one state east and two states north along the Atlantic Ocean. What state am I in?
(Delaware)

I am in Nevada and I travel two states north and four states east. The first letter is M. What state am I in?
(Minnesota)

I am in Missouri and I travel three states east and one state south. The first letter is W. What state am I in?
(West Virginia)

I am in Michigan and I travel one state south. The first letter is I. What state am I in?
(Indiana)

I am in Maine and I travel one state south and one state west. What state am I in?
(Vermont)

I am in New Hampshire and I travel two states south. The first letter is R. What state am I in?
(Rhode Island)

I am in Minnesota and I travel one state south and one state east. The first letter is I. What state am I in?
(Illinois)

I am in North Carolina and I travel two states north. What state am I in?
(Maryland)

I am in New Jersey and I travel five states south. What state am I in?
(South Carolina)

I am in South Carolina and I travel five states north. What state am I in?
(New York)

I am in New Mexico and I travel three states east along the Gulf of Mexico. Then I travel two states north. What state am I in?
(Kentucky)

I am in North Dakota and I travel one state east and four states south. What state am I in?
(Louisiana)

I am in Pennsylvania and I travel one state north and one state east. The first letter is M. What state am I in?
(Massachusetts)

I am in South Dakota and I travel three states south. What state am I in?
(Oklahoma)

I am in New York and I travel one state south and one state west. Then I travel one state north. The first letter is M. What state am I in?
(Michigan)

I am in Ohio and I travel two states west and three states south. What state am I in?
(Mississippi)

I am in Rhode Island and I travel two states north. The first letter is N. What state am I in?
(New Hampshire)

I am in Tennessee and I travel one state east. What state am I in?
(North Carolina)

I am in Oklahoma and I travel one state north and one state west. What state am I in?
(Colorado)

I am in Wisconsin and I travel five states west along the Canadian border. What state am I in?
(Washington)

I am in Texas and I travel five states north. What state am I in?
(North Dakota)

I am in Virginia and I travel three states south along the Atlantic Ocean. Then I travel four states west. The first letter is T. What state am I in?
(Texas)

I am in Oregon and I travel one state south along the Pacific Ocean. Then I travel two states east along the Mexican border. What state am I in?
(New Mexico)

I am in West Virginia and I travel five states west. The first letter is U. What state am I in?
(Utah)

I am in Utah and I travel one state east and one state north. The first letter is W. What state am I in?
(Wyoming)

I am in Washington and I travel one state east and one state south. The first letter is N. What state am I in?
(Nevada)

I am in Vermont and I travel two states east. What state am I in?
(Maine)

I am in Wyoming and I travel two states west. The first letter is O. What state am I in?
(Oregon)

I am in Montana and I travel one state east and three states south. The first letter is N. What state am I in?
(Nebraska)

I am in Indiana and I travel five states east. The first letter is C. What state am I in?
(Connecticut)

HOME PET HOME

Objective

To recognize two main parts of an address—the street name and the building number—and locate places on a map using addresses

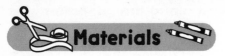 **Materials**

♦ **Pet City Map (page 49)**

♦ **Pet Cards (page 50)**

♦ **Crayons**

♦ **Scissors**

♦ **Paste**

Before You Start

1. Ask students, "How can you tell your own home from a neighbor's home?" *(Responses may include a description of their home, the location of landmarks such as a fire hydrant or a lamppost near their home, or the street address.)*

2. Tell students that the most helpful way of locating a house is by its street address. Explain that an *address* is made up of the building number and a street name.

3. Ask students where they might find the number of a house. *(On the house or on the mailbox)* Where would they find the name of a street? *(On street signs or on the mailbox)*

4. Point out that families who live in an apartment house have another number or letter in their addresses to tell exactly which apartment they live in.

5. Tell students that addresses are important so that they can find places, such as their school or a friend's house. Ask students why it might be important for them to know their own address. *(To get help if they are lost, or to direct someone to their home)*

Note: *Caution students against giving their addresses to people they don't know.*

To Do

1. Give each student a copy of Pet City Map and Pet Cards. Have students color and cut out the pets.

2. Next, have students paste each pet on the correct home using the addresses on the Pet Cards.

3. When everyone is finished, you may wish to go over the game with the class. Call on volunteers to explain how they knew where to paste each pet.

Name: _____

**Look at the neighborhood map below.
Paste each pet at the correct address.**

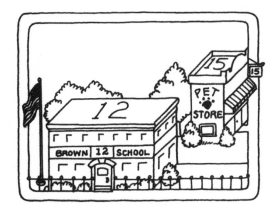

APPLE WAY

CHERRY STREET

ORANGE LANE

PEAR DRIVE

Name: _____

PET CARDS

Color and cut out each pet.

Then paste each pet at the correct address on Pet City Map.

12 Apple Way

15 Apple Way

32 Cherry Street

15 Pear Drive

42 Pear Drive

14 Orange Lane

15 Orange Lane

49 Cherry Street

WHICH ROUTE SHOULD I TAKE?

Objective

To locate places on a map and follow routes to get to the places

Materials

- **City Map (pages 52–53)**
- **Find-a-Route Cards (pages 54–55)**
- **Scissors**

Before You Start

1. Ask students how they get to school each morning. Responses might include walking or coming by car, school bus, or public transportation. Tell students that the way they get from their home to school is called a *route*. It is a way of getting from one place to another.

2. Invite students to describe how people might use maps to plan their routes to get to places. Explain that planning a route on a map makes it easier to get to places.

3. Show students the City Map and invite them to identify places on the map.

4. Point to I-Love-to-Learn Elementary School and then point to the Friendly Fire Station. Ask a volunteer to come up and trace a path from the school to the fire station.

5. Now point out the cardinal directions that are written along each side of the map: North, East, South, and West. Have the same student retrace the route from the school to the fire station using cardinal directions and street names.

6. Explain to students that the best way to find a route on a map is to locate the place where they will begin and where they will end up and then trace a path between the two places.

7. Tell students that they are going to play a game in which they must find a route from one place to another on the map. Students must use cardinal directions and street names to play the game.

To Do

1. Divide the class into groups of four or five. Give each group a set of Find-a-Route Cards and the City Map. Stack the Find-a-Route Cards face down next to the map.

2. Decide which player goes first. Pick a card from the pile and read it aloud. If the player describes the correct route from one place to another using cardinal directions and street names (for example, to get from Delicious Deli to the Amusing Museum, go west on Hyacinth Place), the player may keep the card. If not, place the card at the bottom of the pile.

3. The player that collects the most cards at the end of the game wins.

Going Further

Have each student create one game card to add to the deck of cards.

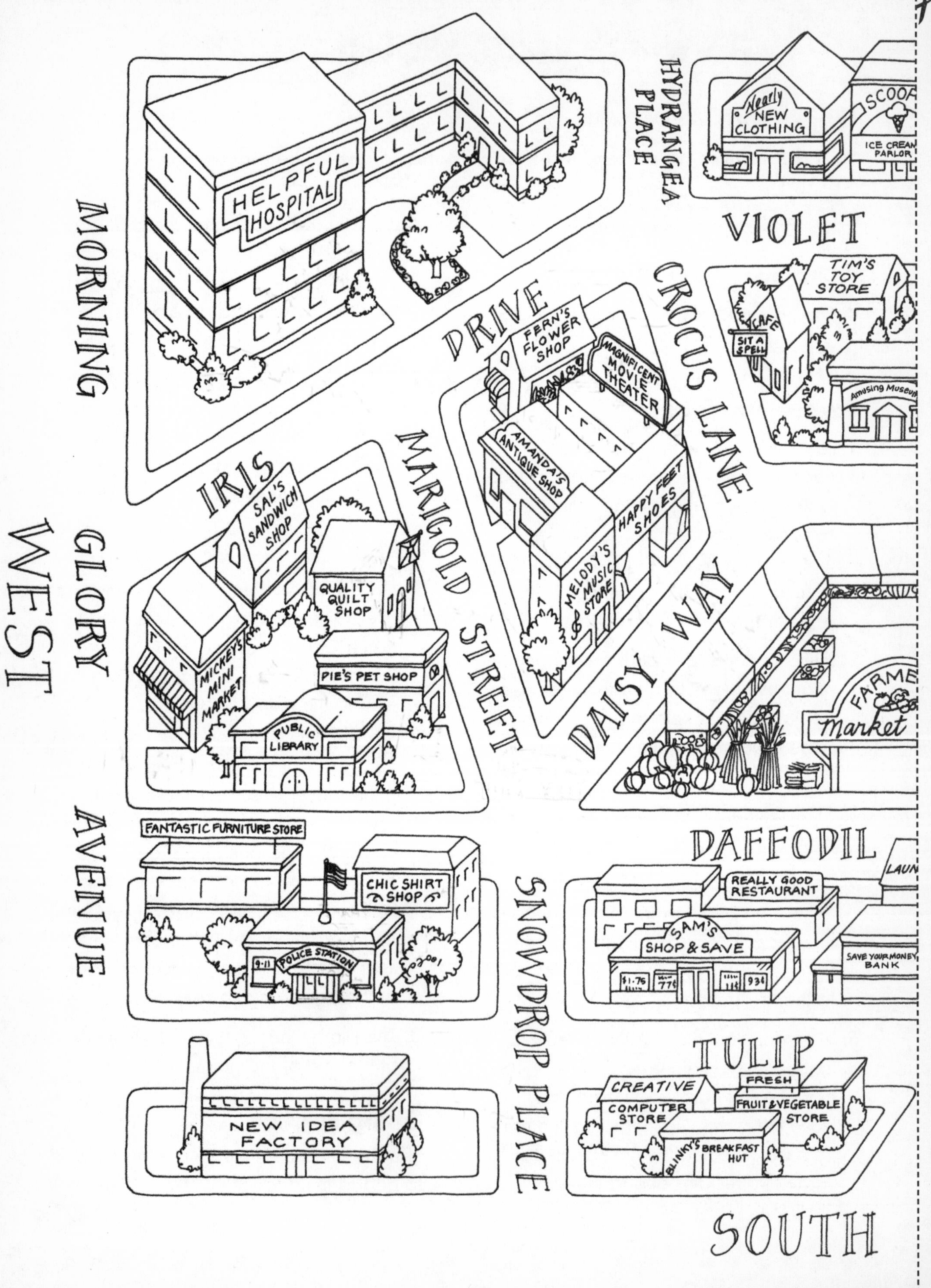

HELPFUL HOSPITAL
MORNING
GLORY
WEST
DRIVE
HYDRANGEA PLACE
Nearly NEW CLOTHING
SCOOP
ICE CREAM PARLOR
VIOLET
CROCUS LANE
TIM'S TOY STORE
CAFE
SIT A SPELL
Amusing Museum
FERN'S FLOWER SHOP
MAGNIFICENT MOVIE THEATER
AMANDA'S ANTIQUE SHOP
HAPPY FEET SHOES
MELODY'S MUSIC STORE
IRIS
MARIGOLD STREET
SAL'S SANDWICH SHOP
QUALITY QUILT SHOP
MICKEY'S MINI MARKET
PIE'S PET SHOP
PUBLIC LIBRARY
DAISY WAY
FARMERS Market
AVENUE
FANTASTIC FURNITURE STORE
CHIC SHIRT SHOP
9-1-1
POLICE STATION
SNOWDROP PLACE
DAFFODIL
LAUN
REALLY GOOD RESTAURANT
SAM'S SHOP & SAVE
$1.75
77¢
93¢
SAVE YOUR MONEY BANK
NEW IDEA FACTORY
TULIP
CREATIVE COMPUTER STORE
FRESH FRUIT & VEGETABLE STORE
BLINKY'S BREAKFAST HUT
SOUTH

FIND-A-ROUTE CARDS

Which route should I take to get from I-Love-to-Learn Elementary School to Granny's Gas Station?

Which route should I take to get from Pie's Pet Shop to Squeak's Animal Shelter?

Which route should I take to get from Helpful Hospital to the New Idea Factory?

Which route should I take to get from Manny's Miniature Golf to the Really Good Restaurant?

Which route should I take to get from the Sit-a-Spell Cafe to the Fresh Fruit and Vegetable Store?

Which route should I take to get from Blinky's Breakfast Hut to the Police Station?

Which route should I take to get from the Nearly New Clothing Shop to the Twilight Tower Office Building?

Which route should I take to get from the Fire Station to Scoop's Ice Cream Parlor?

Which route should I take to get from the Fantastic Furniture Store to the Save Your Money Bank?

Which route should I take to get from the Amusing Museum to the Trusty Train Station?

FIND-A-ROUTE CARDS

Which route should I take to get from the Chic Shirt Shop to Fern's Flower Shop?	Which route should I take to get from the Post Office to the Police Station?
Which route should I take to get from Herb's Health Food Store to the Buy a Book Store?	Which route should I take to get from Scoop's Ice Cream Parlor to the New Idea Factory?
Which route should I take to get from the Post Office to Melody's Music Store?	Which route should I take to get from the Twilight Tower Office Building to the park?
Which route should I take to get from the Creative Computer Store to Amanda's Antique Shop?	Which route should I take to get from the Police Station to the I-Love-to-Learn Elementary School?
Which route should I take to get from Sal's Sandwich Shop to the Fresh Fruit and Vegetable Store?	Which route should I take to get from Bunny's Bakery to Pie's Pet Shop?

MODEL TO MAP

Objective

To recognize the difference between a model and a map of the same place

 **Materials**

- ◆ **Model of a School (page 57)**
- ◆ **Map of a School (page 58)**
- ◆ **Crayons and pencils**

Before You Start

1. Give each student a copy of the Model of a School. Explain that a *model* is a smaller version of something, such as a school, and appears 3-dimensional. You can see the upright walls, doors, and furniture.

2. Ask students to name the different rooms that they see in the model—the lunchroom, the gym, the principal's office, the library, three classrooms, and the nurse's office. Invite students to tell what clues they used to identify each room.

To Do

1. Give each student a copy of the Map of a School. Invite students to compare the map with the model. Ask students how they are the same. *(The rooms are the same and their locations are the same.)* How are they different? *(The model looks 3-D, while the map is flat. The map has labels, but the model doesn't.)*

2. Explain that a *map* is a drawing of a place. Tell students that a map can help you find your way around a place, such as a classroom, a neighborhood, or a city.

3. Point out that the symbols on the map key, such as the desks and chairs, represent the real desks and chairs in the model. Ask students what other objects in the model are shown as symbols on the map.

4. Have students cut out the symbols next to the map. These symbols belong in each room on the map. Tell students to use the model as a guide and paste the symbols in the correct places on the map. Invite students to draw additional symbols that they think may be missing.

Literature Link

Mouse Views by Bruce McMillan (Holiday House, 1991).
A class's pet mouse escapes from his house and goes on a tour of the school.

Name: _____

MODEL OF A SCHOOL

Color in the model of a school.

MAP OF A SCHOOL

Cut out the symbols and paste them on the map.
Use the model as a guide.

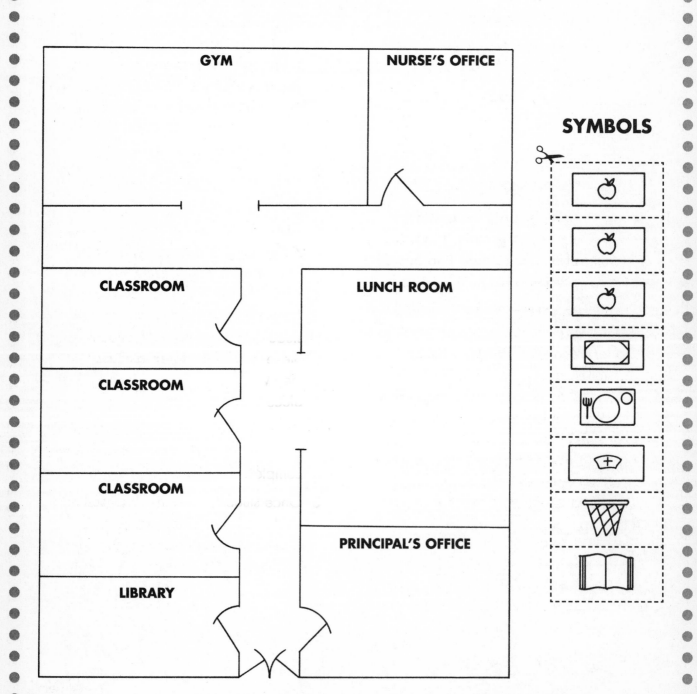

SYMBOLS

PICTURE THIS

Objective

To use a grid map to uncover a mystery picture

 **Materials**

- ◆ **Picture Grid (page 60)**
- ◆ **Mystery Picture (page 61)**
- ◆ **Scissors**
- ◆ **Paste**
- ◆ **Crayons**

Before You Start

1. Draw a grid map on the board that is five columns by five rows. Label the columns from left to right 1 to 5, and the rows from top to bottom, A to E.

2. Explain to students that a *grid map* is a kind of map that is divided by lines to form squares. Each square is assigned a letter and number to help readers find places on the map. Show students the letters running down the left side of the grid and the numbers running across it. Point to the square on the upper left-hand corner of the grid and tell students that this square is A-1.

3. Draw a circle in square C-3 and ask if anyone can name the square in which the circle is located. Point to row C and then run your finger across the row counting out loud as you move from C-1 to C-2 to C-3. You may want to repeat this several times until students become more familiar with the process.

To Do

1. Give each student a copy of the Picture Grid and Mystery Picture. Have them cut out picture A-1 and paste it in the correct location on the Picture Grid. It is very important that students cut and paste one picture piece at a time to their grid map so they won't forget where each picture piece should go.

2. You may wish to challenge students to guess the mystery picture before they complete the grid map.

3. Once students have finished pasting all their picture pieces to the grid map, have them color in their pictures.

Name: _____

PICTURE GRID

	1	2	3	4	5
A					
B					
C					
D					
E					

| | 1 | 2 | 3 | 4 | 5 |

MYSTERY PICTURE

Cut out one picture piece. Paste it in the correct box
on the Picture Grid. Continue cutting and pasting one piece
at a time until the picture is complete.

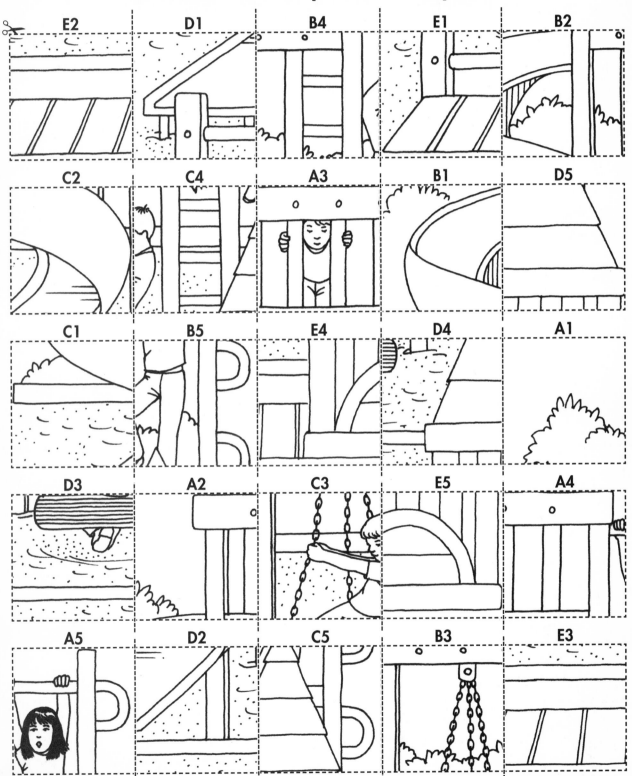

ANIMAL FARM GRID MAP

Objective

To understand how to read a grid map and use it to locate things

Materials

◆ **Barnyard Grid (page 63)**

◆ **Farm Animal Cards (page 64)**

◆ **Crayons**

◆ **Scissors**

◆ **Glue or paste**

◆ **Pencil for each student**

◆ **One small sheet of paper for each student**

Before You Start

1. Review what a grid map is and how it works. Draw a grid map on the board that is four columns by four rows. Label the columns from left to right, 1 to 4. Then label the rows from top to bottom A to D.

2. Draw a circle in square B-4 and ask if anyone can name the square where the circle is located. Point to row B and then run your finger across the row, counting aloud as you move from B-1 to B-2 to B-3 to B-4.

To Do

1. Give each student a copy of the Barnyard Grid and Animal Cards. Have them color and cut out the Animal Cards. Then have them paste each animal onto a square of the Barnyard Grid.

2. Group students into pairs. Each player must guess where his or her partner's animals are pasted. Without looking at the partner's board, each player takes a turn calling out a grid-map square (for example, B-2).

3. If a player succeeds in naming a grid square where his or her partner has pasted an animal, the player gets another turn until he or she misses. If the player does not locate an animal, the partner takes a turn.

4. Players should keep track of the grid squares that they call out on a separate piece of paper. The first player to find all their partner's animals wins.

Literature Link

Family Farm **by Thomas Locker (Dial, 1988).**
A family finds a way to earn money to save the family farm.

BARNYARD GRID

Name: _____

FARM ANIMAL CARDS

Color and cut out the animals below.
Paste each animal in a different square
on the Barnyard Grid.

Sheep

**Sheep and
3 lambs**

**Cow and
calf**

**Hen and
2 chicks**

**Pig and
2 piglets**

**Duck and
3 ducklings**